THE BEANO BOOK OF AMAZING ANIMALS

Senior Editor
Belinda Weber

Senior Designer
Sarah Goodwin

Designer
Nina Tara

Design Assistant
Rachel Fuller

Publishing Director
Gillian Denton

Author
Anne Gatti

Artwork Archivists
Wendy Allison
Steve Robinson

KINGFISHER
An imprint of Kingfisher Publications plc
New Penderel House
283-288 High Holborn
London WC1V 7HZ

First published by Kingfisher Publications plc 1998

2 4 6 8 10 9 7 5 3 1

A CIP catalogue record for this book is available from the British Library

ISBN: 0 7534 0292 0

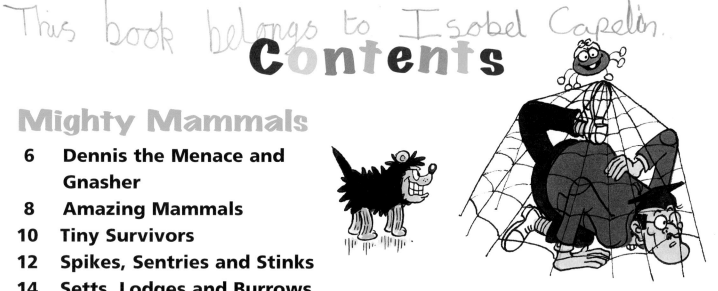

This book belongs to Isobel Capelin.

Contents

Mighty Mammals

Beautiful Birds

Wriggly Reptiles and Amphibians

Into the Deep

Creepy Crawlies

Amazing Mammals

MOST OF THE giants of the animal world are mammals, just like Dennis the Menace and Gnasher. Having furry coats and being able to make their own body heat allows mammals to live in extremely cold spots as well as in hot places. All mammals have backbones and they all feed their babies on milk – even the two egg-laying mammals, the platypus and the echidna.

▼ OUCH!

A baby giraffe has a bumpy birth – the mother has her baby standing up and the youngster drops nearly 2m to the hard ground – that's the height of a grown man. Still, the hardy youngster can stand up and run with the herd in about 20 minutes.

▲ GORILLASPEAK

Most of the time gorillas feed peacefully together in the trees. But babies quickly learn that adults, especially males, do not like to be stared at. A yawning male might also be looking for a fight.

▲ NOSE POWER

An elephant's trunk is a brilliant tool. It uses it for washing, for picking up signals, for pushing and carrying things and as a snorkel when it is swimming.

▲ TAKE THAT!

Tigers are the biggest of all the cats and are amazing hunters. They are so strong that they can knock their prey off balance with a single swipe of a paw! They usually attack from the side or behind.

◀ LONG HORNS

The female rhino's front horn is the longest single horn in the world. It can grow to more than 1.5m (about 3 times as long as a human arm). She uses it to protect her baby and to dig up roots to eat.

▼ MEGA MEALS

The blue whale, the heaviest animal on Earth, eats some of the tiniest creatures in the sea, called krill.

 It doesn't feed when it travels or when it's breeding, but the rest of the time it needs to swallow about 4 million krill a day!

Tiny Survivors

THE GOOD THING about being tiny, as the pygmy shrew (the tiniest land mammal in the world) knows, is that you can crawl into something as small as a worm's hole when you're being chased. Remember that, Ivy! Some small mammals can make speedy getaways, while others hide underground.

Actual Size

▲ BIG EARS
Bats find their food in the dark by sending out high-pitched shrieks – as many as 200 per second – and listening to the returning echoes that bounce off objects such as flying insects.

▲ LITTLE SHREW, BIG APPETITE!
Shrews have the biggest appetites of any mammal. They scoff their own weight in insects and worms every day. To eat this much, they have to eat every couple of hours.

▼ SWIMMING UNDERGROUND
The mole can dig a tunnel 13 times the length of its own body in about 12 minutes. It anchors itself with its back legs, then makes swimming strokes with its front paws.

▲ STRETCH AND GRAB
Bush-babies have big ears and listen for insects at night. When a moth flies by, the bush-baby stands up on its branch and grabs the unsuspecting insect in mid-flight with its hands.

Actual Size

▲ A TASTY SNACK?

Fancy a dormouse sandwich? The Romans used to eat edible dormice, like this one. And one of their cookery books even gives a recipe for stuffed dormouse!

▶ TURNING HEADS!

The tarsier has huge eyes to help it find its food in the dark. It can also swivel its head through 180 degrees, so it can track its insect prey wherever they go.

◀ GROWING UP PRICKLY

A hedgehog's spines are really special hairs. When it is born, the spines are soft and have to harden. Most adult hedgehogs have about 5,000 needle-sharp spines to deter predators.

Spikes, Sentries and Stinks

MAMMALS ARE ARMED with various weapons, from horns and spikes to tusks and hooves, for self-defence. Some have hidden weapons which come as a nasty shock to the attacker and even Gnasher would be wary of a zorilla. For others, like gazelles, having super-sharp senses help them make a speedy getaway.

▶ WHAT A STINKER!

Skunks squirt a foul-smelling liquid at their attackers. The smell can be so vile that it makes people sick, and it can be smelled up to 2.5km downwind. The oily liquid clings to the attacker's fur and can last for days.

▼ A SUDDEN FLASH

Impala can leap a record-breaking distance to escape cheetahs. Some jump up to 11m – the human long jump record is just 8.8m. The sudden flash of white on the impala's rump warns others to flee.

▲ SPIKE ATTACK

The crested porcupine's first line of defence is to raise its pointed quills, stamp its feet and grunt. If that doesn't work, it reverses into the intruder – prickles first. Ouch!

▲ SOLID BALL

The pangolin looks a bit like a spiky pine cone. It has a coat of overlapping scales, which makes excellent armour. The underparts of its body are soft, so when a predator comes near, the pangolin rolls itself into such a tight ball that it can't be prised open by a person or hungry attacker.

▶ REAR ATTACK

The zorilla's weapon is a stink bomb. When an enemy gets too close it lifts its tail and fires a stream of smelly, stinging liquid at its face.

▼ CIRCLE OF HORNS

Adult musk oxen use their huge shaggy bodies as a windbreak when the winter blizzards set in. They make a tight circle around any young, with their curved horns at the ready. If any wolves did attack, they would meet a full grown adult head-on!

13

Setts, Lodges and Burrows

AN UNDERGROUND HOME is one of the safest a small mammal can have. Ivy the Terrible might like to investigate living underground when things get too tough above ground. Expert builders like beavers use both their teeth and claws to make their homes sturdy enough to last several years. Some mammals are expert at being lodgers – they let other creatures do all the hard work.

◀ ANCESTRAL HOMES

Badgers get very attached to their setts which have several chambers. They spring clean them by dragging their bedding outside on dry mornings. Some families use the same sett for 200 years or more – and they may even have a few lodgers.

▲ NO FRONT DOOR

The harvest mouse splits blades of grass with her teeth to make her ball-shaped nest high up on a stem. She is so light – she weighs the same as a 2p piece – that she can scramble through grass without breaking any stems.

Home Sweet Home

The world's biggest burrower is the Australian wombat (about the size of a badger) which can excavate 3m of soil in an hour.

The largest badger sett ever measured had 50 underground chambers and 178 entrances.

The most crowded mammal homes are the caves used by female free-tailed bats in Texas, USA. In one of these caves, 10 million females gave birth (one baby each) over 10 days.

▲ TREE HOUSE

A strong, thick branch makes a fine home and larder for a leopard. It drapes any extra food over the branch, out of reach of lions and hyenas.

▼ WATER ENGINEER

Ask a beaver if you want some tips on housebuilding. Using just its teeth and claws, it makes itself a waterproof chamber inside a tent-sized mound of logs and mud, called a lodge.

Friends and Relations

S OME ANIMALS, LIKE a solitary polar bear, live alone for most of the time, only meeting up when they want to mate. But many others have a better chance of finding food and a good place to live if they stick together – so take note, Bash Street Kids. Being one of a gang, with the extra protection that offers, can mean having a longer life, too. In winter, some birds huddle together for warmth, keeping each other cosy and snug.

▶ STRIPEY SIGNALS

When ring-tailed lemurs jump down on to the forest floor to look for food, they keep in touch with each other by holding their long tails straight up like a flag.

▲ BROTHERLY LOVE

For male cheetahs, it's really important to grab a territory and hold on to it. Brothers often team up – some stay together for life. They run at incredible speeds – they can go from a standstill to 96km/h in just three seconds, making them the fastest sprinters.

▼ GIRL POWER

In elephant herds, it's the females who rule. The head of a herd is always a female. It's her job to find the group food and water. She's also their chief protector, but the other females help her – standing by her side, facing outwards, they'll make a tight circle around any baby elephant that's in danger.

▲ CLOSE RELATIONS

It's hard to believe, but the closest ancestor of the rabbit-sized hyrax is the elephant!

What do you call a lot of lions?

A pride.

What do you call a lot of geese?

A gaggle!

What do you call a lot of Bash Street Kids?

A nuisance!

▲ A BITING BOSS

The silvery-maned male is the boss of a hamadryas baboon family. If a female wanders away, he barks at her and then bites her on the neck to remind her how to behave!

▼ BIG DADDY

In a lion family, called a pride, the male is the protector. His deafening roars can be heard up to 8km away. Males protect their own cubs, but if a new male takes over the pride, the newcomer usually kills the cubs and mates with the females.

SWIMMING IN CIRCLES

Dolphins are brilliant at team work. When they find a shoal of fish, they split up and swim round the fish, herding them into a circle. Then they charge in and snap them up.

Tongues, Teeth and Standing on Tiptoe

CLAWS AND PAWS are used by many mammals to grab food, as Chester the cat knows, but tongues can work surprisingly well, too. The giraffe has the longest and one of the most mobile tongues in the animal world. The giraffe and gerenuk chew their food but another tongue user, the aardvark, simply swallows it whole. The vampire bat also swallows its liquid food – blood! – but it needs teeth to bite into its animal victim.

▲ MEAL OF BLOOD
It takes about half an hour for a vampire bat to lap up enough blood to make a nourishing meal. It bites its victim with needle-sharp teeth and a chemical in its saliva stops the blood from clotting. It has to eat about half its body weight in blood each day to survive.

▶ STICK FINGERS
The aye-aye, a cat-sized lemur, has an extra long middle finger. It listens for grubs moving about inside tree bark, then gnaws a hole and scoops them out with its twig-like finger.

▼ MORE OF THE SAME
The giant panda takes a long time over its meals – in fact it chomps away on bamboo leaves for over 12 hours every day. It has an extra pad on each of its front paws to help it grip the smooth bamboo stalks.

◀ SLURP AND SWALLOW
An aardvark can rip open a termite mound with its powerful claws. Then, it pokes in its long sticky tongue and pulls it out, covered in termites which it swallows whole.

▼ TONGUE-TASTIC!

The giraffe's tongue is almost as long as a person's arm. It can curl it round leaves growing on thorny branches and pull them off – leaving the prickly bits behind!

▼ BALANCING ACT

Juicy leaves are food and drink to the gerenuk. To reach them, it stands on its back legs, resting the front ones on a branch for balance.

Babyminding

WHEN MOST MAMMALS are born they are small and helpless – although you might not believe this, looking at Ivy! The mother feeds them on her rich milk, cleans them and keeps them warm. Some mothers, like kangaroos, are on duty for months. Others only have to suckle for a couple of weeks. Mammals that live in family groups often help each other look after the young.

▲ BABY COMES TOO

The lesser bush-baby mum takes her baby with her when she goes out looking for food at night. She parks it in a tree close to her hunting spot, and the baby clings on tight until she comes back.

◀ A BOUNCING BABY

When a baby kangaroo is born, it is the size of a bee. Luckily it can stay in its mother's comfy pouch for six months or more while it grows strong. When it's older, it often dives back in if there's danger about.

▲ FREE MILK

It's easy for a baby capybara to get a meal. It lives in a nursery with lots of other babies and any of the mums will give it milk if it asks nicely!

◀ FOLLOW MY LEADER

Baby cheetahs stay with their mother for almost two years. They follow her white-tipped tail through the long grass.

Can I have a Teddy Bears' picnic, Mum?

Of course, Ivy. That sounds nice!

Funny. Ivy's toys are all in their box.

IVY'S TEDDYS

Ivy! Get these baby bears back to the zoo!

Aw, Mum! We're having great fun!

ZOO

◀ UNDERGROUND TOWNS

Prairie dogs live in groups called townships. Adults stand on their back legs and watch over the young. They bark a warning if there is any danger.

▼ RIDING PIGGY-BACK

Baboons live in big groups of up to 200 animals, called troops. Young baboons keep up with the crowd by riding around on their mother's back.

▲ MEGA-FAMILIES

Mice have large families with up to six or seven babies in a litter. Some females raise a new family every four weeks.

Shrew Train

When a mother white-toothed shrew goes hunting, she takes her babies along too. Each youngster holds on to the backside of the one in front. They have such a strong grip that if you were to lift the mother, her babies would dangle in a long line below!

Snowy Wastes and Scorching Deserts

MAMMALS CAN LIVE in deserts and snowy lands. In deserts, they survive by spending the hottest part of the day out of the heat, often in cool underground burrows. Snow dwellers have thick coats and a layer of fat, like Fatty Fudge when he's dressed up for winter. Many of them grow special winter shoes and a white coat that makes it tricky for predators to spot them.

▲ SNIFF AND DIG

In the freezing winters, reindeer travel south, where the snow is softer, and dig down with their hooves until they find clumps of lichens. Scientists think they can smell the plants through the snow.

▼ SNEAKY HUNTERS

A polar bear's white coat provides great camouflage against its snowy background. Only its nose is black and some researchers have reported seeing polar bears covering their noses with their paws when stalking seals on the ice.

▼ SPEEDY SLURPER

A camel can go for a week in the scorching desert without a drink. When it does drink, it gulps down up to 60 litres (that's over 105 pints!) in just a few minutes.

▲ SNOW GRIP

In autumn, the snowshoe hare puts on its snowshoes – it grows thick pads of long hairs on the soles of its feet which help it get a grip in the deep snow and stop it from sinking into snowdrifts.

▼ A HOT SOAK

The winters are very cold on the island where the Japanese macaque lives. Luckily there are hot springs there so the monkeys just climb in and wallow in the warm water.

25

Amazing Birds

ALL BIRDS HAVE feathers and lay hard-shelled eggs. Feathers help to keep them warm and are used for flying. But even those birds that can't fly have feathers. Taking care of their feathers is an important job and a lot of time is spent making sure they are clean and in perfect condition. Minnie the Minx would never cope with all that washing! Birds live everywhere, but most are found in jungles, where there is plenty of food and shelter.

This special duck caller should attract a duck!

DUCK RESERVE

QUACK! QUACK!

It's working!

QUACK! QUACK!

Bah! Smiffy drives me quackers!

QUACK! QUACK!

▲ TAWNY TALK

When tawny owls are out at night, they chat to each other. One bird makes a 'too-wit' sound and the other replies 'too-whoo'.

26

▶ HUGE SOUNDBOX

The crane's windpipe is a whopping 1.5m long. It is coiled up inside its neck, and helps to make the bird's trumpeting calls extra loud.

▼ BIG BEAKS

Toucans have huge, bright beaks which are incredibly strong. They use them to pluck fruit and berries from trees.

▼ JUNGLE SHOWOFFS

The male bird of paradise lifts up his wings to show off his great train of brightly coloured tail feathers. Some males also do frantic dances on the branches and some hang upside down to impress the females.

▼ IN A FLAP

Hummingbirds beat their wings incredibly quickly – about 80 times per second. This high-speed flapping makes a low humming sound.

Bird of paradise

Hummingbird

Toucan

Flying Machines

MOST BIRDS CAN fly but some are much better at it than others. Large birds with broad wings, like vultures and eagles, can soar for hours. Some birds are expert at hovering – they beat their wings really fast to stay exactly in the same spot. Ocean gliders have long narrow wings and steer with their tail feathers. What type of flyer do you think Fatty would make?

WING POWER

When the albatross stretches out its wings, they are longer than a hatchback car. Gliding across the ocean, it can cover the distance from the north of Scotland to the south of England in a day.

▲ MEGA FLIGHT

Swifts are amazing flyers. They even sleep in the air. But they have weak legs and can't walk or perch very well. They really only land to raise their young, at the age of about two. That means that swifts can fly non-stop for some 500,000km – that's the same as twelve and a half trips around the world.

▼ HOVERSPEED

Hummingbirds can beat their wings so fast that all you see is a blur of feathers. They can keep flapping a million times without stopping.

Winged Wonders

The peregrine falcon is the fastest animal in the world. It can clock up speeds of up to 200km per hour when it dives – that's almost twice as fast as the maximum speed allowed on motorways.

The highest flying bird ever known is a Ruppell's griffon that collided with a plane over Africa at 11,277m.

Not counting birds that hover, the slowest flying birds are two kinds of woodcock which flap along at 8km per hour without stalling.

Hummingbirds are the best twisters and turners in the air. They can fly forward, backwards, sideways and upside down as well as hover and spin.

◀ TIRELESS TRAVELLER

The Arctic tern spends so much of its life travelling, that it would put Billy Whizz to shame! It's incredible journey takes it about 16,000km from its summer feeding grounds to its winter ones. Then it flies back again!

▲ UNDERWATER FLYER

Penguins can't fly in the air but they do fly underwater, using their flippers as wings. Some of them can race along at 27km per hour!

▼ BEEP BEEP

The roadrunner can fly, but it prefers to race along the ground in its desert home. Sprinting along, it has clocked up speeds of 26km per hour – a 10-year-old cycling at top speed would only just be able to keep up! The fastest vehicle is Thrust 2 which holds the land speed record of over 1,000km per hour.

Roadrunner

Ostrich

29

Weavers, Tailors and Builders

When it comes to making a nest, some birds take after Gnasher and make an untidy pile of sticks and plants. Then they simply lay their eggs on top. Others are perfectionists like Walter the Softy and spend days weaving grass into a small fortress which they line with soft feathers or moss. Some male birds, like wrens, make several different nests and allow the female to choose the one she likes best.

▶ A BIT PECKISH

Long-tailed tits' nests have domed roofs. They line their nests with feathers and moss, bound together with spiders' webs. The young are fed caterpillars and each parent may have to make 500 journeys a day to feed the hungry offspring.

▲ A WOVEN HOME

Using his beak and feet, the male weaverbird ties grasses around a forked twig and threads them over each other until he's made a tightly woven nest with a porch at the bottom.

▲ A GOOD EGG!

The ostrich is the world's biggest living bird and, not surprisingly, lays the biggest eggs – about 24 times the size of a hen's egg. The shell is so strong that it can support the weight of an adult man, but the baby ostrich can crack it when it is ready to hatch.

▶ SEWING KIT

The tailorbird uses her beak as a needle and strands from a cobweb as thread to sew together two or three leaves to make a hanging nest. It takes her four days to finish it.

▶ FISHY THROATS

Baby pelican chicks search for regurgitated, partly digested fish in their parent's pouch. They catch their own food when they are about 10 weeks old.

▲ DEVOTED DAD

The male Emperor penguin is a champion balancer. He stands in the freezing winds on the Antarctic ice for two months, keeping the egg warm by resting it on its feet.

31

Feeding Tools

BIRDS USE THEIR beaks and feet for feeding – and no-one tells them off! Imagine what Dennis' mum would have to say if he tried to eat with his feet. Thin, delicate beaks, like a hummingbird's, are excellent for poking inside flowers to get at the nectar. Strong, hooked ones, like an eagle's, can tear prey into pieces. Birds that catch insects in the air often have tiny beaks but their mouths are huge.

▲ EATING INSIDES

There's a good reason why some vultures are bald – they eat the soft bits inside a dead animal. Head feathers would get very bloody, very quickly.

▲ SPIKING A FISH

Slippery fish are no trouble for a fish eagle – it has spikes on the underside of its talons. It grabs a fish from under the surface of the water and keeps a firm grip on it until it reaches the shore.

▼ BIG MOUTHS

Pelicans have a pouch of stretchy skin under their beaks. They scoop up about a bucketful of water and fish, squeeze out the water and swallow the fish whole!

▲ EATING UPSIDE DOWN

Flamingoes turn their heads upside down and swing them through the water, sucking in water and trapping tiny creatures on a fringe of small hairs inside their beaks.

◀ RUN RABBIT, RUN

The golden eagle has long sharp talons for toes and a hooked beak for gripping its prey and tearing it into manageable bits.

33

Staying Alive

ALTHOUGH BIRDS ARE quite safe when they are flying, they make easy targets for mammals, reptiles and bigger birds when they're on the ground or in a nest. Les Pretend would like the ptarmigan, which uses camouflage to keep out of sight. Others rely on tactics like producing foul smells to keep predators away.

▲ STINK BOMBS

Both the mother hoopoe and her chicks obviously don't mind living in a stinking home. When they are in the nest, they produce a stench like rotting meat from a gland near their rear end to keep nosy-parkers away.

▼ HIGH SECURITY HOMES

The world's smallest owl, the elf owl, has discovered that the stems of giant cacti make excellent shady homes. A bonus is the spines, which keep the predators out.

▲ BLENDING IN

There aren't many places to hide when the Arctic lands are blanketed in snow but the ptarmigan makes itself almost invisible by moulting its speckled brown summer feathers and replacing them with white ones.

▼ SEEING RED

The male robin gets furious when it sees red feathers. It usually means another male is trying to move in on his territory and that always means trouble.

It's pouring. Wear your waterproof coat, Ivy!

It'll keep you nice and dry!

That's what Mum thinks!

What's the point of rain if you can't get soaked in it?

SPLASH!

◄ FOOLED YOU

A hungry fox is a real threat for baby plovers. But Roger would be proud of their mum. She leads the fox away by fluttering on the ground, pretending to have a broken wing. When the fox is away from her babies, the plover flies off.

▼ LEG POWER

Never insult a cassowary. It can't fly, but it can kick out like a martial arts expert and it has dagger-like claws on its feet, which are strong enough to rip open someone's body!

SLIPPERY SLIDERS

Penguins may look clumsy on their feet, but they can slide! They can push themselves over the ice at great speed, sliding on their bellies.

Amazing Reptiles and Amphibians

REPTILES, LIKE SNAKES, lizards, crocodiles and tortoises are tough skinned or horny. Sunbathing is a must for them – a reptile can't keep up a steady body temperature by itself, so it needs to be warmed by the sun before it can start moving about, rather like Smiffy on his summer holidays! Sun-baked places are a problem for amphibians like frogs, toads and salamanders, as they must always keep their skins moist. Most of them need water to breed in, too.

▲ SLOWLY DOES IT

The tuatara is a reptile that once roamed about with dinosaurs. Its low body temperature makes it a real slowcoach – sometimes, it even falls asleep in the middle of chewing its food!

▼ TEARFUL TURTLES

Turtles really cry. When they eat sea plants they swallow gulps of saltwater too. Too much salt will kill them, so they get rid of it by crying salty tears.

▼ NOISY WARNING

Rattlesnakes have a rattle, made of horny segments, at the end of their tail. They shake it as a warning to intruders. The rattle can be heard 30m away.

▲ GOING UNDERGROUND

The spadefoot toad burrows underground with its heels. The cool, damp soil stops it from drying out in hot weather. If there's a drought, it can stay buried for as long as 11 months.

▼ CARING MUMS

Nile crocodiles are great mothers. The female buries her eggs in the sandy riverbank. When they are ready to hatch, the babies call from inside the eggs, and the mum scrapes away the sand. Then, she gently picks the hatchlings up with her teeth – each baby is 4,000 times lighter than its mum – and carries them to the river.

Lures and Ambushes

CHASING A MEAL is a tiring business and many reptiles prefer to lie in wait. They either hide or use camouflage to make themselves invisible – a trick that Roger might find useful. Some snakes can even ambush in the dark, using special cells that detect the warmth given off by another animal. Some creatures use bits of their bodies to trick small animals into coming near them.

▲ A SNAPPY SNACK

When a crocodile grabs its prey from the riverbank, its jaws snap shut with the force of a 13-ton clamp! As the croc can't chew its food, it spins the dead animal round and round in the water, to tear off bite-sized chunks of flesh.

▲ WHAT A BIG MOUTH!

The grass snake can slide into a pond and grab a frog in its jaws. It carries the frog back to land and swallows it whole.

◄ WRIGGLY TONGUES

The alligator snapping turtle has a tongue that looks like a worm! When it is hungry, it opens its mouth wide. Passing fish swim in, mistaking the wriggling tongue for a tasty worm.

FANCY A CUDDLE?

The boa constrictor's patterned skin helps to camouflage it as it lies in wait on tree branches. When it spots its dinner, it drops down on to its victim, and squeezes it to death.

Silently, the Gnash hound creeps up on his prey!

CRAWL!

HIGH-SPEED TONGUES

Chameleons are ace ambushers. They can change the colour of their skins to blend in with their backgrounds and their tongues are amazing weapons. In less than one second, a chameleon can shoot out its tongue, hit a bug with its sticky tip and whip it back into its mouth.

A REAL DRAGON

More like a shark than a dragon, the Komodo dragon hides in bushes, waiting for wild pigs or deer. It grabs its prey and rips it apart with its saw-like teeth.

He waits for the exact moment to strike!

RUSTLE!

Good job bowls of dog food can't run away!

GNASHER'S GNOSH

Fangs and Poisons

FOR AN ANIMAL that has no claws and can't run or jump, a pair of fangs which squirt deadly venom is a brilliant weapon. Minnie the Minx finds a squirt of water works just as well! Many snakes strike their prey, injecting them with a lethal dose, then simply wait for them to die. For small, soft-bodied creatures like toads and frogs, having poisonous skin is a great way to stop being eaten.

▲ I TASTE BAD!

Salamanders protect themselves by having poisons in their skin. The fire salamander's brilliant colouring warns hungry predators of its bad taste and suggests that they give it a miss.

▶ HANDLE WITH CARE

Touch the skin of a poison-arrow frog and you could end up dead! There are 60 kinds of these cheery looking hoppers in South and Central America. The local bush people used to use the poison to coat the tips of their arrows when hunting.

◀ SHOULDER SPRAY

The cane toad keeps its venom in bulging sacs on its shoulders. It can spray this venom into the eyes of an attacker from up to 1m away.

► HOW CHARMING!

You may think a snake likes the music of the snake charmer but actually it can't hear it! Snakes are deaf and follow the movement of the flute, which they think may be an enemy, about to attack.

Frog Facts

Did you know that there is a smelly frog? The Venezuelan skunk frog lives in the cloud forests of the Andes. Its defence is not a poisonous skin but a foul smelling one.

The smallest amphibian in the world is the Cuban frog. It grows to just 1.2cm in length – smaller than an adult's thumbnail.

The largest amphibian in the world is the Goliath frog from Africa. It can grow to up to 30cm long.

▼ MONSTER LIZARD

When the gila monster defends itself, it bites into its enemy and chews hard to make venom swill up through its bottom teeth and into its victim's flesh.

▼ SUPER FANGS

The king cobra has fangs that are long enough and strong enough to pierce the hide of an elephant. With just one bite, it can inject enough venom to kill this giant mammal in just four hours.

43

Tricks and Bluffs

BILLY WHIZZ CAN always make a speedy getaway but many reptiles and amphibians can't move quickly enough to outrun their enemies. Instead they use various tricks to confuse or fool their attackers. Making a sudden change to the shape or size of their bodies is a favourite one. Pretending to be something else – or even dead! – can also baffle a predator.

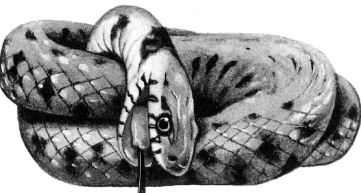

▲ WHAT AN ACTOR
One way of getting out of a tight fix is to play dead. The European grass snake even makes its tongue hang out of its open mouth to look really dead.

▼ SCARY NECK
The Australian frilled lizard is a formidable fellow. It has a frill of skin around its throat which usually lies against its back. If the lizard is threatened, it rears up on its back legs, raises its frill and hisses at its attacker. Many large predators are frightened off, even though the lizard is harmless.

▼ LIZARD SNACK

If a fox is getting too close for comfort, a lizard can snap off its own tail and make a getaway, leaving the tail as a snack for the surprised fox.

▶ DON'T SPIT!

Can you spit accurately from more than 3m away? Well, the spitting cobra does, in self-defence. If the spit gets in a person's eyes it burns and can even make them blind for a short while.

▶ MOBILE HOMES

Tortoises protect their soft bodies with a tough shell. If they are threatened by a predator, they retreat inside their shells, pulling in their legs, tail and head so they can't be eaten.

Running and Gliding

I'T'S STRANGE TO think of reptiles and amphibians taking to the air, but several frogs and geckos and even one snake do as a nifty way of changing trees. Roger might be tempted to try flying as a way of dodging his homework. In deserts, snakes use muscle power to get across the sand, while some lizards have fringes on their toes which help them to get a grip on the sand.

▶ HOT STUFF

The sidewinder wriggles across burning hot sand, keeping most of its body off the ground. It only touches the sand in two places, looping, sideways and forwards, with the rest of its body.

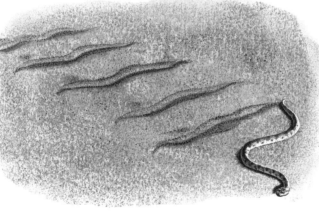

▲ WALKING ON WATER

The basilisk is an extraordinary animal – it can run on water! If it is threatened, it rears up on to its back legs and starts running. When its long-toed feet hit the water, they create a cushion of air which stops it sinking.

▲ A NEW SKIN

Reptiles, like the banded gecko, shed their skins and grow new ones as they get older. They rub themselves against sharp stones to tear off the dead skin, revealing a new one underneath.

▼ FLYING FROG

The flying frog can make spectacular escapes from predators by leaping off a branch and gliding for up to 45m – the width of a school football pitch – to another tree. The webbed skin between its toes acts like a parachute.

Amazing Sea World

SEA CREATURES, FROM the tiny animals that drift near the surface to the biggest animal on earth (the blue whale), live in all parts of the world's oceans, even the deepest bit (the cold, dark Marianas Trench in the Pacific). But most of them live in the top 200m. Just like on land, there are hunters, vegetarians, crawlers, sprinters, travellers and stay-at-homes. And Roger could certainly learn a new dodge or two from some of these devious characters.

▼ TUG OF WAR

The starfish has a great knack for getting things to come out of their shells! It latches on to a shellfish and just pulls!

▼ SMART AMBUSHER

The octopus is one of the smartest animals in the sea. It ambushes its food using a special trick – it can change the colour of its skin to blend in with its background!

▲ MASTER OF DISGUISE

The blotchy wobbegong shark has a seaweed-like fringe around its mouth. This makes it look like a weed-covered rock.

Octopus

Starfish

▶ CITY AFLOAT

The Portuguese man-of-war is not one animal but millions of tiny sea creatures all working together to survive. They form a kind of floating city and each creature takes on one role to help the whole community. What would happen if the Bash Street gang tried this? Scary stuff!

◀ CRACK SHOT

The pistol shrimp kills its prey by shooting them with a blast of sound that is so loud it can shatter glass. The noise stuns the prey, then the shrimp darts in and eats it.

▼ LIVING CARPET

The plaice lies flat on the bottom of the seabed. It disguises its shape by disturbing the mud or sand so that it settles over its fins. This breaks up its outline, making it harder for a predator to see it.

▼ GRUMPY FISH

A moray eel is a bad-tempered fish with a very big mouth. It lurks in crevices watching for passing crabs which form most of its diet.

Plaice

Moray eel

Underwater Escapes

IN ROCKY PARTS of the sea, hiding is a favourite way of escaping from predators. Ivy usually finds this works! Another is having camouflage. But many sea creatures arm themselves with poisons or weapons like spines. Others, like flying fish, make dramatic getaways.

► SPIKY MOUTHFUL

When threatened, a porcupine puffer fish swallows water to blow itself up into a balloon shape.

▼ CAN'T CATCH ME!

Huge side fins and a powerful tail help the flying fish to make its amazing getaway. It flicks its tail to propel itself out of the water, then spreads its fins and lifts into the air. It can 'fly' at up to 65 km per hour for over 200m before dropping back into the water.

▲ ROOF GUEST

A hermit crab makes an easy snack for an octopus, but not when it has a sea anemone, with long, stinging tentacles, living on top of its shell home. The crab gets protection and the anemone gets free travel.

▼ WEEDY SHAPE

The sea dragon is a weird shape for a good reason. It lives in beds of kelp plants and its seaweed-like fronds make it almost invisible.

Watery World

A starfish can leave behind an arm or two as it escapes from a predator. It then regrows them.

A cuttlefish squirts out a screen of brown inky stuff while it makes its escape. Photographers used to use this ink to print their photos.

The death puffer is the most poisonous fish in the world. Just a small amount of poison can kill. Even so, the Japanese eat it as a delicacy after they've cut out the poisonous parts!

▶ COLOUR CODED

Even soft-bodied, slow-moving animals such as sea slugs can protect themselves. Their bodies are brilliantly coloured which tells predators that they are poisonous to eat and are best avoided!

53

World of the Coral Reef

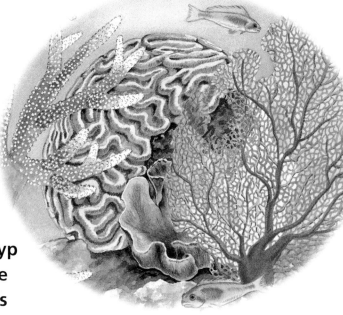

CORAL REEFS, WHICH grow in warm, unpolluted seas, are the jungles of the sea world. Tiny animals, called polyps, live together in colonies known as corals. What would a Bash Street coral look like? Each polyp makes a chalky cup and these cups form huge rocks, with the polyps on the surface. There is plenty of food for the huge number of animals that live in these colourful sea jungles.

▼ COLOURFUL CAMOUFLAGE

Many of the fish that live in the coral reefs are brightly coloured. Their bold patterns blend in with the colourful corals.

Angel fish

Lion fish

Parrot fish

Butterfly fish

Cowfish

▲ BIGGER AND BIGGER

This coral is called brain coral because it looks like the human brain. More and more polyps grow until they form a huge colony, which would easily fill a football goal.

▼ A STINGING HOME

Most small fish steer clear of the stinging tentacles of the sea anemone but clown fish can even sleep there without being stung. In return for this safe home, the clown fish chases away anemone-eaters, like butterfly fish.

▼ NOSING ABOUT

A slim body and a long, thin, nose enable the butterfly fish to squeeze into cracks between the rocks and suck out any small creatures that are hiding there.

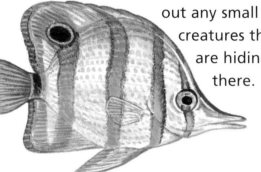

▶ STONE LOOKALIKE

The stonefish has bumpy, mottled skin which makes it almost impossible to spot when it is lying on the seabed. It waits patiently for a fish to swim by, then snaps it up in its big mouth.

▶ DART AND POUNCE

It may look clumsy, but an octopus can dash out of its hiding place to ambush prey, propelling itself along by squirting water out of a tube behind its head. It can also crawl along the seabed, gripping with the suckers on its tentacles.

Living in the Deep

EVEN IN THE deep-sea zone of the sea, where it is very cold and dark, there are fish, shellfish and other creatures like urchins, snails and sea cucumbers. Over half of these deep-sea dwellers have parts of their bodies that light up – some flash on and off, others shine all the time, a neat trick, eh Dennis? The animals use these lights to find mates in the dark, to lure prey or to confuse predators.

▶ **OPEN WIDE!**
The viperfish has about 300 spots inside its mouth which light up. It hunts with its mouth wide open, so that the lights dazzle and confuse its prey.

I'm a deep-sea fish, swimming through the inky, black depths!

And my battery's run out!

GOING FISHING

Bacteria light up the weird fin on the angler fish's forehead. When curious fish swim up to investigate, the angler drops its huge jaw and the fish are sucked in.

EYE SPY

This squid spends its life in the dark waters of the deep-sea zone One of its eyes is four times bigger than the other.

AT THE READY

The hatchet fish has a large, upturned lower jaw and eyes that can look upwards. These help it to catch some of the tiny animals that sink from the surface.

SWINGING LURE

The deep-sea dragon has a long streamer dangling from its chin with glowing bacteria at the end. It swings it through the water to attract other fish.

CHEEK LIGHTS

This deep-sea fish has glowing bacteria in its cheeks which act like a car's headlights, lighting up the way ahead.

Freezing Waters

THE CREATURES THAT live in the Arctic and the Southern Ocean (the seas round the icy land of Antarctica) spend much of their time under a roof of ice. But there is a surprising amount of food for them, from tiny plant plankton to shellfish, fish and squid. Not even Fatty Fudge would go hungry. In the Southern Ocean penguins have to watch out for the leopard seal and killer whales. In the Arctic, seals and walruses are still hunted by humans.

▲ STICKING YOUR NOSE OUT

When the Southern Ocean freezes over, the Weddell seal gnaws through the ice to make itself air holes. When it needs to doze off, it puffs out its throat to keep itself floating.

▶ WHALE MEALS

A seal makes a really good meal for a killer whale. They have even been seen tipping up an ice floe to knock a basking seal into the water.

▲ HANDY WHISKERS

When the Arctic freezes over in winter, it becomes pitch dark on the seabed. No problem for the walrus, though. It uses its moustache of about 500 whiskers to feel for shellfish in the mud.

▶ WATCH YOUR STEP

Adelie penguins seem to know that leopard seals stay close to the icy shore of the Antarctic. When they need to go hunting, they stand at the edge and peer down for signs of the enemy. If the coast is clear, they dive in and swim away at high speed.

▲ CORKSCREW WEAPON

The male narwhal grows a corkscrew-shaped tusk out of its top lip, that sticks out like a lethal, 2m-long skewer. It uses it in fights with other males.

59

60

Amazing Bugs

NO-ONE, NOT EVEN Teacher, knows exactly how many kinds of bugs there are in the world, but at least 80 per cent of the known types of animals are arthropods – they have skeletons on the outside, jointed legs and a body that's divided into segments. Spiders, millipedes, crabs and insects are all arthropods. Because they are so small, these animals can live in a variety of places. Most insects, which include flies, beetles, ants and grasshoppers, have wings and can escape from predators quickly.

▲ HAIRS FOR EARS

The male silk moth's antennae are like giant feathers. Each one is made up of about 17,000 hairs which can pick up the scent of a female silk moth.

◀ FLASHING FIREFLIES

Fireflies and glow-worms produce their own light. In some countries, people used to keep them in cages to light up their rooms.

◀ SWEET AND SOUR

A blowfly is one of the many flies that sucks nectar from flowers. It also has a taste for rotting flesh and can smell a corpse from up to 35m away – that's like from the top of a four-storey building.

◄ HEARING LEGS!

Grasshoppers keep their ears on their legs! Special receptors on the legs pick up sounds and alert the grasshopper if danger is approaching. If disturbed, a grasshopper can leap high into the air to escape. If its attacker grabs hold, the grasshopper will sacrifice a leg to get away.

▲ MID-AIR CATCHES

A dragonfly can catch minute midges in the air because it is a high-speed flyer and has excellent eyesight. Each bulging eye is made up of over 1,000 lenses, and they cover almost its whole head.

Weird Bits

ONE THIRD OF all animals in the world are beetles. Fireflies, weevils and ladybirds belong to the beetle family too, so it's not surprising that many of the strangest shaped bugs are beetles. Perhaps Plug was a beetle in another life! Some have outsized noses, other have jaws that look like horns or claws. Many insects have bulging eyes which make them look a bit like Martians, but allow them to see all the way round.

▼ WHAT A NECK

The giraffe-necked weevil has a neck that's twice as long as its body. Rival males use them in head nodding contests – the one that nods the longest is the winner.

▼ BALLOON BELLIES

The job of some of the ants in the honeypot colony is to store food in their bodies. When there is plenty of food, they are fed huge amounts, but when food is scarce, other worker ants stroke them to make them give up their bounty.

▶ ALL-PURPOSE TOOL

The pincers at the back of an earwig's body make a very useful tool. The earwig can use them to grab prey, in self-defence and in courting and mating. The female's pincers are straight, the male's curved.

◀ LONG HORNS

Hercules beetles have very long horns which can measure more than half the total length of the beetle. Fighting males use their horns in wrestling matches, where each one tries to flip the other on to his back.

▼ FEEDING TOOL

Nut weevils have amazingly long snouts – some are almost as long as the beetle's body. Their tough jaws are at the tip.

▲ BIG HEAD

The goliath beetle, with its huge, bulky head and armoured body, is the heaviest insect in the world. It weighs about the same as three house mice.

Traps and Attacks

BEFORE BUGS CAN use their fangs, claws or jaws to kill their prey, they have to catch them. Calamity James would have all sorts of problems! Many bugs are expert ambushers. Once one of these killers spots a moving meal, it pounces out of its hiding place, which can be a specially built trap or simply a twig or leaf that's the same colour as its body. Then it's grab, crunch and swallow.

▼ A SLIPPERY END

The antlion larva makes a cone-shaped pit in its sandy home and then buries itself at the bottom. A passing bug slips into it, but before it can scramble out, the speedy antlion grabs it with pincer-like jaws and sucks out its body juices.

◄ LISTENING LEGS

At night the trapdoor spider pokes its head and front legs out of its underground burrow. The hairs on its legs pick up the movements of other bugs so the spider knows when to pounce.

▶ WATCH YOUR STEP!

When a bug walks across the roof of the purse-net spider's home, the spider instantly stabs it with its long fangs and drags it underground to eat it. Later, it repairs the hole and waits for the next bug to stroll by.

LOOK OUT BELOW!

Hanging above the ground from a thread, the net-throwing spider holds its web in its legs. When an insect comes into range, it drops its sticky net and hauls up its dinner!

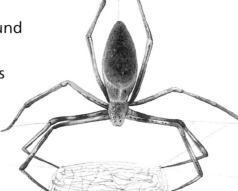

▼ LIGHTNING STRIKE!

The praying mantis looks like a twig as it sits dead still on its perch. When a bug moves into range, it takes just one-twentieth of a second to spear the unlucky bug in its spiky forelegs.

SPIDERY FACTS

There are about 40,000 kinds of spider and all of them are venomous. About 30 kinds are poisonous to humans – the worst being the Brazilian huntsman. Fortunately there is an antivenin, so very few people die from its bite.

Spider silk is the strongest fibre in the world. A strand of spider silk is 250 times finer than a strand of hair! But it is twice as strong as the same thickness of steel.

Some young spiders travel by parachute. They climb to a high spot, spin a thread of silk and wait for the wind to blow them to a new place.

The largest spider in the world is the goliath bird-eating spider from South America. With its legs outstretched, it is the size of a dinner plate!

▶ ASSASSINS

Assassin bugs are so-called because of the speed and ferocity with which they attack their prey. They grab a bug with their strong forelimbs, then suck out its juices.

Har! Har! I'm going to make a trap for Dad!

Just make sure it's not too strong!

Who trapped you, Minnie?

ME! BAH!

Disguises and Surprises

BUGS OFTEN PROVIDE easy-to-get food for other animals. But some bugs have fascinating survival techniques – they are superb mimics, they wear disguises, they give their predators nasty surprises or they make speedy getaways – Dennis would probably try all of these at once! Many bugs are poisonous and they often announce this by being brightly coloured.

▼ ROLL UP, ROLL UP

A millipede's best way of defending itself is by curling into a tight coil so that its soft parts are protected by the tough shell. Some brightly coloured millipedes also give off a foul-smelling poison.

▶ LEAF MIMIC

Some leaf insects look just like crinkled leaves. Others, like this one, mimic fresh ones. They even sway from side to side, as if they were caught in a breeze.

TAKE AIM, FIRE!

The bombardier beetle makes a mixture of burning chemicals inside its body and then fires them out through the tip of its abdomen. It can direct the spray forwards or backwards and to either side of its body!

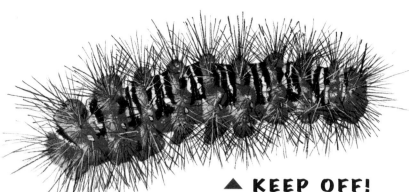

▲ KEEP OFF!

It's hard for caterpillars to defend themselves, but some kinds sprout hairs that are either poisonous or barbed. Their bright colours warns predators not to try to eat them.

Creepy Caterpillars

Each full-grown caterpillar of the yellowtail moth is covered with up to 2 million irritating hairs.

The caterpillar of the citrus swallowtail butterfly looks just like a fresh bird's dropping.

▶ EYE TRICK

If a lizard or a bird moves in on this brown cricket, it flicks open its wings which are patterned with red and white spots that look like huge eyes. This startles the predator, giving the cricket time to hop away.

▶ THORNY DISGUISE

By sitting still on a thorny stem, this treehopper, which is shaped and coloured like a thorn, escapes being spotted by a sharp-eyed bird.

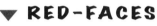

▼ RED-FACES

If the puss moth caterpillar is threatened, it rears up and waves its red head at the attacker. If this doesn't put it off, it squirts formic acid.

Dad's Boss is coming to visit!

RRING!

My Boss! He's here!

How dare you greet me in disguise! Argh!

Hardworking Parents

BUG PARENTS OFTEN work really hard to make sure their eggs are in a safe place, close to a good supply of food for when the grubs emerge. Sometimes this means boring into a hard material like wood or hiding the eggs in specially built shelters. But for most bugs, the parents' job is done once the female has laid the eggs – lucky for Plug, he's not a bug! The earwig is one of the few insects that babyminds.

▲ CLAY NURSERY

The potter wasp mum makes a real clay pot for her egg, stocks it with fresh food in the form of a caterpillar that she has paralysed, then seals it for safety with a clay plug.

▼ DUNG BALLS

Pushing a ball of dung along backwards to bury it in a safe place is hard work for a beetle. But it's worth it, as once the beetle has laid an egg in it, the ball makes a nutritious nursery for the grub.

▲ TIME TO GO

The female earwig is a perfect mum (well, almost). She stays with her eggs, cleaning and turning them until they hatch. Then she guards them for another week or two. After that, if they don't leave, she may well eat them!

▶ DRILLING INTO WOOD

The female long-horn beetle searches for a hard log that has not yet started to rot. Then she drills a hole, using her powerful jaws, and drops in a single egg so that it's hidden from view.

▲ SAFE RIDE

Baby scorpions are pretty helpless: their skins are soft and their stings are blunt. The mother makes a ramp out of her pincers so the youngsters – up to 90 of them – can climb on to her back and they stay there until they harden and sharpen up.

Working Together

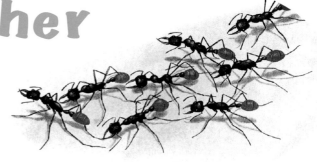

JUST TAKE A look at what insects can do when they work together in a group. They can build the largest homes, in terms of their size, of any creature in the animal kingdom; they can make air-conditioned hives where 1,500 eggs are laid each day; they can kill and carve up animals hundreds of times bigger than they are. Minnie would like the fact that the head of many of these insect groups is a queen, whose main job is to lay eggs. The other members have specific jobs, too.

▲ MASSIVE ATTACK

Worker army ants have jaws like garden shears. Protected by soldier ants, raiding parties set out to find food. They attack any animal in their path – they have even been known to kill a tied-up dog – and carry the pieces back to the nest.

▶ WORKERS AND BODYGUARDS

Leafcutter ants chop off pieces of leaf and carry them back to the nest to make compost for the fungus food they grow. Small workers go with them as bodyguards, to see off any flies that might try to lay their eggs on the leafcutters while they are transporting their loads.

▶ JOB LIST

There are up to 80,000 worker bees in a large nest and a worker's job changes as it gets older. At first it is a nurse, feeding the grubs; then a builder and repairer, using wax from its own body; then a guard; and finally a food finder, bringing back nectar and pollen from flowers.

▼ EATING MACHINES

It is so dry where desert locusts live that usually only a few of the female's eggs hatch to become hoppers. But after heavy rains, more and more hatch and survive. When they have eaten all the food nearby, they fly off in a vast swarm of up to 50,000 million. In just one day, the swarm can strip an area of crops that would feed 500 people for a year.

▲ MUD TOWERS

Thousands of tiny termites work together to build huge towers of mud, cemented together with their saliva. The tallest ever found was 12.8m high – over 2,000 termites would have to make a ladder out of their bodies to reach the top. The tallest building made by humans is about the height of 250 people.

Amazing Pets

DOGS AND CATS have been living with humans for thousands of years as their pets. It's easy to see why – they can be useful, good company, fun to stroke and play with. But people keep all sorts of other pets, including snakes, insects and lizards, which are not exactly cuddly. These need very special care and housing and most of them don't like to be handled. Their owners find it fascinating to watch the way they move, feed and behave.

TEETH LIKE SAWS

Piranhas have a bad reputation. That's because their teeth are sharper than a shark's! They can rip their prey to shreds in just a few minutes. Some people living in the Amazon region used to use piranha teeth to cut wood!

▲ SMART PIGS

Miniature pet pigs, like the Vietnamese pot-bellied pig, are the latest pet craze in America. They are about the size of a terrier and have a short snout and wrinkled face. They can be trained to use cat flaps and litters, and to obey commands. Many owners say they are smarter and sneakier than dogs – but then, they haven't met Gnasher!

Pet Heroes

A mongrel called Chips was one of the most famous dog heroes during the Second World War. When a group of American soldiers landed on the island of Sicily with their mascot, Chips, they were trapped by gunfire coming from a pillbox. As they lay face down on the sand, Chips ran straight towards the pillbox and jumped in. The gunfire stopped, and a few minutes later an Italian soldier came out with Chips, who was clearly wounded, biting his throat and three other soldiers trying to stop him.

Two elderly sisters often fed a seagull they called Nancy outside their home. One day, one sister was walking alone along the cliff top when she tripped and fell. The seagull flew back to her sister and pecked hard on the window. When the sister came out, the gull led her to her injured sister.

▶ ANCIENT PETS

The Egyptians kept pet ferrets almost 5,000 years ago. Although some people don't like their strong smell, ferrets make playful pets.

◀ HAIRY LEGS

Although the tarantula has eight eyes, it can't see very well. It uses the hairs on its legs as feelers, to help it find its way around. If threatened, a tarantula will flick its hairs at its attacker. These irritate and can cause a painful rash.

▶ LONG AND LEAN

The reticulated python, the longest snake in the world, is a slim, beautifully patterned snake. In captivity, it can grow to 7m – that's longer than an estate car. It is quick to attack, so only a skilled snake handler should think of keeping one.

Index